Y0-BRG-032

Wishing You and Your Family a Christmas to Remember

From _____

Let's Make a Christmas Memory

Shirley Dobson
and
Gloria Gaither

WORD PUBLISHING

Dallas·London·Vancouver·Melbourne

LET'S MAKE A CHRISTMAS MEMORY

ISBN 0-8499-5089-9

Printed in Hong Kong

Christmas...
Dobson Style

Shirley Dobson

The Christmas season has always been greeted with great excitement in the Dobson home. The delicious food, the aromas, the gifts, and of course, the worship of the Christ child made that season the most cherished time of the year for us. This is the way I described it in the original edition of *Let's Make A Memory*.

We also set aside a few days before Christmas for baking our traditional cookies and candies, not

only for the family but for neighbors
and friends. This emphasizes to our
children the spirit of giving. As
Ryan says, "I love Christmas
because everyone in the neighborhood is always sharing."

Then comes the special night
when we go as a family to pick out
the Christmas tree. I look for a fir
with the best shape, and Jim looks
for the best price! Having made the
selection, we designate an evening
to add the decorations. Excitement
fills the room as the lights are strung
on the tree and we begin hanging

red balls and dozens of specially selected ornaments that I have collected over the years. The house resounds with traditional Christmas music, and we drink hot chocolate and munch our home-baked Christmas cookies and candies. (Is it any wonder that Christmas is such a fattening time in the Dobson household?)

When our children were younger they each had their own "tree"—a small artificial fir which they decorated with lights and their own ornaments. They have become much too sophisticated to continue the tradition, but their memories of the occasion are still warm and meaningful.

On Christmas Eve, we enjoy dinner of Chinese food each year. (Don't ask me how that tradition started, or more important, why?) Afterwards, grandparents, aunts, uncles, and cousins join us around the fireplace, and Jim reads from the Bible. After discussing the passage, we do something very meaningful. The lights are lowered and I give each family member a votive candle.

I explain as we take our turn igniting
our candle that the light represents
Jesus who was born into a dark
world to give us eternal life. As
each person lights his candle, he
shares one blessing he is especially
thankful for during the past year,
and something he or she is asking
God to do in his life the following
year—perhaps a spiritual goal for
the coming year. We then blow out
our candles and Jim closes in
prayer. The children then get to
select and open one gift from under
the tree.

On Christmas morning, Danae and Ryan open the small gifts in their stockings first; then we have our traditional Christmas brunch, consisting of warm cinnamon rolls, orange juice, and coffee. When the big moment arrives, we sit around the tree, and Ryan and Danae act as "Santa," passing out presents which are opened one at a time in an effort to preserve this happy moment as long as possible.

Finally, we gather at the dining table for our Christmas dinner of turkey, dressing, cranberry sauce, mashed potatoes, two kinds of salads, and hot baked rolls. When we think we can't hold another bite, our traditional dessert of pound cake and ambrosia (a fruit dish prepared with peeled grapes in it) is brought out. The family peels the grapes the evening before the meal. There's always laughter and warm family interaction during the activity. (The recipe for our ambrosia is provided on the following pages, as well as the recipe for our traditional Christmas brunch cinnamon rolls.)

These happy days of Christmas come and go so quickly that we have sought a way to hold on to the pleasure a while longer. Therefore, we have developed a custom of saving our Christmas cards from friends and loved ones far and wide, and after New Year's Day, I put them on a tray near the dinner table. Every night we select four cards, one for each family member, and we read them and the enclosed letters. We then pray for those families around our table. This tradition may take

13

months to complete, depending on the number of cards we receive. With the busy days of Christmas behind us, we can better enjoy the beauty of the cards, and absorb the meaningful verses and personal notes.

The Christmas traditions that we have developed through the years are not unique to the Dobson household. Perhaps yours are similar in many respects. But they are extremely meaningful to each member of our family. These activities serve to emphasize the two vitally important themes that embody the Christmas spirit: celebration of Jesus' birth and life, and celebration of love for one another and for the entire human family. As such, this exciting time of the year brings out the very best that is within us.

What special times those were when our children were young. Of course, they are grown now and we have moved to a new home in Colorado. But much remains unchanged. Our son and daughter join their grandparents in visiting us during the Christmas season.

I still enjoy decorating the house and making it look festive. I love to cook the same traditional foods, although greater attention is paid now to the fat content of some specialties. On Christmas Eve, we will either attend a local church service or have our candle-light ceremony at home. The family togetherness and excitement are easily rekindled, even after so many years.

My point is that we are busily making "new" holiday memories even though our circumstances have changed. That is, after all, one of the richest joys of family life.

CHRISTMAS MORNING BRUNCH CINNAMON ROLLS

(Serves 6)

★ 1 pkg. Pillsbury Crescent Dinner Rolls

★ butter or margarine

★ granulated sugar

★ cinnamon

★ 1 small pkg. crushed pecans

Unroll dough into 4 rectangles (*do not tear apart as in making crescent dinner rolls*). Butter each rectangle generously. Then sprinkle on lots of sugar. Shake cinnamon on top. Add pecans.

17

Roll into small logs and put in refrigerator for 3 minutes. Take out and slice into ¼-inch thick pinwheels. Place on ungreased baking sheet, tucking pinwheel end under roll to prevent its unraveling while baking. Bake according to package instructions. Remove from oven and glaze. Make a powdered sugar glaze to spoon on top while rolls are still warm. Absolutely scrumptious with hot coffee or chocolate, crisp bacon, and scrambled eggs. Merry eating!

AMBROSIA

(Serves 8)

★ 1 large bunch of green grapes
★ 4-6 large oranges
★ 1 large can crushed pineapple
★ 1 cup chopped pecans
★ 3-4 bananas
★ 1 cup granulated sugar
★ whipping cream

Cut each grape in half. Take out seeds and peel off skin. (The men can do this around the table while the women are preparing the meal.) Cut peeling off oranges. Section orange slices and remove all white membrane. Cut each section of orange "meat" in half. Each chunk of orange should be about ¼ inch. Add pineapple, pecans, sliced bananas, and sugar. Mix well. This should be real juicy. Serve in glass dessert dishes with sweetened whipping cream on top. We serve Christmas Ambrosia with pound cake—deelicious!

Christmas
Traditions
to Try

- Start a tree-decorating tradition. Serve the *same menu* each year as you trim the tree. The children will look forward to it. (Menu suggestions: clam chowder and bread sticks; Christmas cookies and hot chocolate; Christmas cake and hot cider.)
- Each Christmas, let each of your children choose his or her *own* tree ornament. When they are grown, their ornaments will have special memories as they trim their own "family tree."
- Each Christmas start a tradition of viewing all the family photographs,

slides, and movies. It's fun to see how everyone has changed, and it stirs warm memories to reminisce about when the pictures were taken.

- On December 1, set up a card table with an appropriate jigsaw puzzle (500–1000 pieces). As guests drop in through the holidays, they will enjoy working on the project. The object is to complete the puzzle by Christmas. Set a date with another family to go caroling in the neighborhood. Close the evening with refreshments.

Jesus'
Birthday
Party

HAPPY BIRTHDAY LORD JESUS

Have a party in honor of Him whose birth we celebrate. Include in the celebration an older person who would otherwise be alone, someone you have just met, a young person away from home, and one or two very special friends such as a pastor or teacher who is important to your family's life.

Some special things to make or do might include:

- Birthday-card place cards.
- A special star-shaped cake with white and yellow icing full of fruit,

to represent the fulfillment of the
seed of promise.

- A table centerpiece of a basket or
  small wooden box of clean straw
  surrounded by small packages made
  to represent gold, frankincense and
  myrrh. Someone might tell about the
  three gifts and what they might have
  represented or how they might
  have been used.

  For example, gold was the most
precious metal symbol of God's
most precious gift. Perhaps this provided the financial means for the trip

Mary, Joseph, and Jesus made to Egypt and for their stay there when they were forced to hide from Herod.

Frankincense and myrrh were important spices used in Jewish rituals as incense and as burial spices. Perhaps these gifts hinted at the fulfillment of the old Law as well as the crucifixion of Jesus that was to come. Someone has suggested that Mary may have kept these precious spices and used them to embalm the body of our Lord thirty-three years after his birth.

Making Christmas Eve Memories

- Take a drive through town or a nearby large city to see the outdoor light displays.
- Read the Christmas story aloud from the Bible.
- Sing Carols around the piano or sing with a favorite Christmas record.
- Have every family member take his turn giving some kind of Christmas performance.

- Attend a candlelight or watch-night service. Make attending this special service an annual family affair.
- Let the children open one gift on Christmas Eve. (Perhaps this gift could be sleepwear to keep the children snuggly and warm on Christmas Eve.)
- Hang stockings (to be filled with such things as small toys, toothbrush, comb or brush, old-fashioned toys such as kaleidoscope, wooden top, jacks, pickup sticks, wooden flute, etc.)
- Serve hot wassail. A suggested recipe is on the next page.

HOT WASSAIL

(Serves 6)

- In the base of a twelve-cup
  percolator put:
  - ★ 1 part cranapple juice
  - ★ 5 parts apple cider
    (unpasteurized)
- In the percolator basket put:
  - ★ 6–8 whole cloves
  - ★ 2 cinnamon sticks
  - ★ 2 tbsp. honey
  - ★ ¼ chopped lemon including rind
- Brew wassail as you normally
would coffee, or you may put spices in

the liquid and simmer in a crock pot
or pan on the stove. Dip with a ladle.
• Serve hot with a sliver of lemon or a
cinnamon stick.

If the family condones belief in Santa,
the children could make a snack to
leave out for him. Another nice tradition might be for Mom and Dad to
have a glass of eggnog together after
the children are in bed and take time
to talk about love, blessings, goals,
etc., or just enjoy a few quiet moments
with each other.

Making Christmas Morning Extra Special

- Take pictures or videotape of the children getting up on Christmas morning.
- Have the children stay in bed until Dad gives a special signal. (He could put a record on the stereo such

as "Here Comes Santa Claus" or
some other Christmas music.)

- Have a short worship time before
  opening gifts. Children could do this
  with parents being the "congregation."
- Have a special Christmas breakfast
  every year. A sample menu might
  include: fried apples, bagels and
  cream cheese; blueberry muffins,
  scrambled eggs and bacon; or dried
  beef gravy on homemade biscuits.
  (Some families serve "chocolate
  gravy" that is similar to chocolate
  pudding, but thinner.)

Christmas Day Reunion

- Gather the family together for a
  reunion at grandparents' home.
  Make it a "bring-in" dinner,

everyone supplying his or her special dish, so that no one has all the work!

- Choose one person to be "Santa" and pass out gifts. This might be the same person each time, or the honor could go to the youngest child or the youngest teenager; or, all could "draw straws" for the honor.
- Celebrate by singing around the piano.
- Listen together as Grandfather or another older family member reads the Christmas story, or recite it together from Luke, chapter 2.

- Before Christmas dinner, put two fresh cranberries on each plate. After the family is seated, pass around a basket and, as cranberries are dripped in, share two ways in which Christmas is special to you. Follow by reading John 3:16, and conclude with prayer.

Christmas
Card
Activities

CHRISTMAS CARD DEVOTIONS

- Each day (or on selected days) use the cards received on that particular day, or have someone pull a specific number of cards from a basket used for this purpose.
- During family devotions, or after singing or Bible study, read the cards aloud.
- Have prayer for the families who sent the cards.
- Hang the cards up for display on the mantel, around a doorway or archway, on the back of a door, or on the Christmas tree.

CHRISTMAS CARD PRAYER LINK

Use Christmas cards as a link to real people and their needs through the Christmas season and the month of January.

- Choose one Christmas card each day from those received. Read the whole card aloud and pass it around the family circle. (Do this at a regular time like bedtime or after supper each night or at breakfast time.)
- Have special prayer together for each person in the family that sent the card.

- Send a postcard to that family to tell them about your Christmas-card prayers and that their card was the one chosen on this day. They will appreciate knowing that your family prayed for their family.

AFTER-CHRISTMAS CARDS

- As Christmas cards come, place them in an attractive container. After Christmas is over and the household is more settled, place the container near the dinner table.
- After dinner, pass the container and let each member of the family choose one card.
- Take turns reading the cards and enjoying their beauty.
- Discuss the family or person who sent the card. Are there any specific problems or needs?

- Close your dinner hour by praying for the families or persons who sent the cards.

Homemade Christmas Decorations

GARLANDS FOR THE HOUSE

Make these garlands on evenings before Christmas to use on your Christmas tree or in your hallway, doorways, or stairway:

• Lifesaver garland
  1. Cut two equal strands of desired length of colorful yarns.

2. String Lifesaver candies loosely on the first strand.
3. Lay the string of candy on a table, making the Lifesavers lie flat, in one direction, end to end.
4. With the other strand of yarn weave in and out in the opposite direction so that each candy is forced to lie flat.
5. Secure ends of each yarn to last candy on each end.

- String Cheerios or other circular cereal pieces in the same way, using brightly colored yarn or ribbon. Be prepared to replace the garlands as they are nibbled away.

- String raw cranberries and popcorn alternately onto a piece of yarn.
- String colored marshmallows randomly or in a pattern of colors.
- Make a garland of white foam packing squiggles. Watch that children do not put these in their mouths.
- String uncooked elbow macaroni and other pasta, painting it if desired.

HINT: Dip the end of the string or yarn in melted paraffin to make a "needle" which will be stiff and yet bend.

TREE AND PACKAGE ORNAMENTS

Take a special evening to create these ornaments to use as tree or package decorations.

- Cut shapes from cardboard and cover with foil or glitter.
- Hang sour gumdrop-type fruit slices with ornament hooks that have been inserted in the top of the candy.
- Hang white-chocolate-covered pretzels.
- Wrap popcorn balls in foil or colored cellophane. Secure the wrapping with bright yarn, leaving the ends

long enough for tying the balls onto the tree.

* Make cornstarch clay ornaments. This clay can be molded into shapes and vessels, or rolled on waxed paper and cut with cookie cutters. When dry, it can be painted. (NOTE: This mixture is not to be eaten, but is intended for crafts only.)

CORNSTARCH CLAY ORNAMENTS

Ingredients:

★ 2 cups baking soda

★ 1 cup cornstarch

★ 1¼ cups cold water

Combine all ingredients in saucepan until smooth. Bring to boil and boil one minute, stirring until clay is the consistency of mashed potatoes. Pour out onto a tray and cover with a damp cloth until cool. Knead lightly. Use immediately or store, wrapped airtight, in refrigerator. Warm to room temperature before using.

1. While dough is warm, divide it into two portions. Use food coloring to color one red, the other green.
2. Roll dough on waxed paper and cut into Christmas shapes with a cookie cutter.
3. Poke a large nail through the top of each ornament to make a hole for hanging.
4. Dry thoroughly, turning ornaments occasionally.
5. If desired, glue glitter to parts of ornaments.

DECK THE HALLS

- Cover a large styrofoam ball with sprigs of mistletoe and hang it in an archway or doorway as an excuse for family hugs and kisses. As the mistletoe dries, take care to pick up any berries that may fall, as these are poisonous and may be ingested by small children.
- Have the family make a special time of arranging the nativity set.
- Tie ripple ribbon on the ends of cellophane-wrapped mints, then tie them onto a styrofoam wreath.

- Make homemade taffy. Wrap in waxed paper bits and twist ends. Tie on tree or styrofoam wreath with yarn or string.
- Make large letters out of newspaper or construction paper spelling out "HAPPY BIRTHDAY, JESUS." Tape to large front window.
- Have each member of the family whittle from balsa wood a "Christmon" (Christ-monogram) to hang on the tree, such as a fish, cross, manger, star, lamb, etc. Talk about the meanings of the chosen symbol.

MAGAZINE CHRISTMAS ART

- From old magazines, tear pictures or ads that are mostly green.
- Cut the ads or pictures into pairs of strips of varying measured length, for example, 8 inches, 7 inches, 6 inches, 5 inches, etc.
- Turn a rectangular piece of poster board or construction paper so that the shorter sides are the top and bottom. Draw a vertical line from top to bottom midway between the left and right sides. Starting at the bottom with the longest strips of

paper, glue one end of strips of
equal length to each side of the
vertical line (see diagram). As you
add successive layers of shorter
and shorter strips, slightly overlap
the strips to avoid
having the poster
board or con-
struction paper
show through.

GROWING COLLECTION

As a part of the Christmas celebration every year, give each child an ornament of his own. When the children grow up and move into their own homes, they will have their own ornaments to take with them. These ornaments

might be different for each child each
year:

- ★ crystal
- ★ straw
- ★ wood
- ★ metal
- ★ fancy designer ornament
- ★ handmade

This collection is more than
Christmas ornaments. Rather it is a
collection of special memories,
touched and treasured through the
years.

Memories of a Special Christmas

Gloria Gaither

If everything special and warm and happy in my formative years could have been consolidated into one word, that word would have been *Christmas.* So, by the time the building blocks of my days had piled themselves into something as formidable as late adolescence, Christmas had a lot to live up to.

Christmas, by then, meant fireplaces and the bustle of a big excited family, complete with aunts, uncles, and cousins. It meant great smells from the kitchen—homemade bread

and cranberries bubbling on the
stove, pumpkin pies and turkey. It
meant Grandma's cheery voice
racing to be the first to holler
"Christmas Gift!" as we came in the
door. It meant real cedar Christmas
trees, handmade foil ornaments, and
lots of secrets. It meant enfolding in
the arms of our great family the
lonely or forsaken of our village who
had no place to go. It meant all the
good and lovely things we said
about Christmas being in the heart
and the joy being in the giving.

Then came that other year.

There were many things that
conspired, as it were, to bring me to the
laboratory situation in which I would
test all my so glibly accepted theories.
Grandma was gone, leaving in my
heart a vacuum that wouldn't go away.
My sister was married now and had
the responsibility of sharing her holidays with her husband's people. The
other relatives were far away. After a
lifetime of serving in the ministry,
Daddy had that year felt directed to
resign his flock without other pastures

in mind and "wait on the Lord." Since
I was away at college, just beginning
my first year, I wasn't there when my
parents moved from the parsonage to
the tiny cottage at the lake which a
concerned businessman had helped
them build. Nor was I prepared that
winter day for the deserted barrenness
that can be found in resort areas built
only for summertime fun.

There was no fireplace. There
was no bustle of a big excited family.
Gone was the sense of tradition and
history that is the art of the aged to

provide, and gone was the thrill of the immediate future that comes with the breathless anticipation of children.

The dinner was going to be small, for just the three of us, and there just wasn't any *ring* in the brave attempt at shouting "Christmas Gift!" that Mother made as I came in the door. Daddy suggested that because I'd always loved it, he and I should go to the woods to cut our own tree. I knew that now, of all times, I could not let my disappointment show. I put on my boots and my cheeriest face

and off through the knee-deep snow we
trudged into the Michigan woods. My
heart was heavy, and I knew Mother
was back at the stove fighting back
the tears for all that was not there.

There was loveliness as the forest
lay blanketed in its heavy comforter of
snow, but there was no comforter to
wrap around the chill in my heart.
Daddy whistled as he chopped the
small cedar tree. (He always whistled
when there was something bothering
him.) As the simple tuneless melody
cut through the silent frozen air, I got

a hint of the silent burdens adults
carry, and for the first time felt myself
on the brink of becoming one. So as I
picked up my end of the scraggly, dis-
appointingly small cedar, I also picked
up my end of grown-up responsibility.
I felt the times shift. I was no longer a
child to be sheltered and cared for and
entertained. My folks had put good
stuff in me. Now as I trudged back
through the snow, watching the back
of my father's head, the weary curve of
his shoulder, his breath making
smoke signals in the morning air, I

vowed to put some good stuff back
into their lives.

The day was somehow different
after that. We sat around our little table
stringing cranberries and making foil
cut-outs. But this time it was not the
activity of a child, but sort of a cere-
monial tribute to the child I somehow
could never again afford to be, and to
the people who had filled that child-
hood with such wealth and beauty.

Christmas
Gift
Ideas

- A rustic basket or wooden box (cheese or fruit box) lined with a colorful old-fashioned print and filled with spools of thread, bias tape, straight pins, needles, a thimble, seam ripper, tape measure, buttons.
- A handmade glasses case (leather, felt, needlepoint), filled with cleaning solution for glasses, Sight-Savers, glasses repair kit.
- A carpenter's extra long tape measure, a level, and a square (be sure metric measurements are included).
- A set of metric wrenches.

- A basket filled with shoe polish in basic colors, silicone protecting spray, shoeshine brush and cloth, shoestrings.

- A stocking full of stockings; knee socks for girls, athletic socks for boys, pantyhose for women, dress socks for men. Tie stocking shut with a bright ribbon.

- A small tin tub lined with straw. Inside the tub pack a glass of homemade jelly and a matching glass containing a homemade spicy candle. A square of gingham tied

with ribbon over the top of each jar
will add color and personality.

- Several large bars of Ivory soap, a
  small craft knife, and a booklet on
  soap carving.
- A whole set of toothbrushes and
  toothpastes—one for each member
  of the family. (Be sure each person
  gets a different color brush.) These
  may be packed in a small shoebox
  wrapped in solid color paper. Cut a
  big smile from red and white paper
  to put on the top of the box, or paint
  a smile directly on the box.

GIFT OF TIME

- Each person gives a "gift of time" to every other member of the family. For example: a boy could offer to vacuum the carpet for his mom on the day of her choice; or a father could promise to take his son fishing at some future time.

- Write these time pledges on 3" x 5" cards and place them in envelopes for each person. The envelopes can then be hung on the Christmas tree and opened with other gifts.

KEEPING THE SECRET

To keep the contents of a package secret, place the wrapped and properly tagged package inside a larger box. Pad with newspaper or tissue so there will be no rattling. Wrap outer package and label with another person's name. Do this with as many packages as you wish. When packages are unwrapped, the inner gift is given to the right person to open. Everyone will enjoy *both* surprises! (If you do not want to have to wrap two packages, try making a "quiet" package noisy by adding a few buttons or dried beans, or a light package heavy by adding a rock or other heavy object.)

Over the River and through the Woods

TIME TO REMINISCE

Most children have very little knowledge of their grandparents' earlier years, yet this background offers one of the richest sources of tradition and identity within a family. Children love to listen to the folklore and the stories that grandparents spin so well, and intergenerational discussions reward everyone with meaningful moments of family history, fun, and love. To give your children this important historical perspective and family bonding, spend one evening during your holiday visit listening to the grandparents share their reminiscences of earlier years. Gather the whole family group together after the evening meal in front of the fireplace for a time of listening as the older generation talks.

Before grown children arrive for a visit, get out things you made together or collected as they were growing up. Have these things displayed in a special room. Some things might be: baby books and scrapbooks, sports or achievement awards, report cards, medals, first baseball uniforms, first ice skates, etc.

THE FAMILY THAT PLAYS TOGETHER

When the family clan is together, make time for play. Try any or all of the following:

- Table games such as Scrabble, Strategy, Rook, Trivial Pursuit, Monopoly.
- Puzzles (large time-consuming jig-saw puzzles

offer a wonderful opportunity for
conversation).

- Outside games such as kickball,
softball, volleyball, tennis, bad-
minton, etc. (that is, if you live in a
year-round warm-weather climate).
- Ditch-um (This is a team version of
hide-and-go-seek played at night
from a "home base." Since the
"seekers" are a team, young children
can team up with the grownups and
feel safe.)
- Roller skating party (on the side-
walks in your neighborhood, on a

large driveway, at an empty parking
lot, or at a roller rink).
- Sledding party (with hot chocolate
  and a warming bonfire).

There's no better time than the
holidays to make lasting memories
with your precious family. So . . . have
a wonderful Christmas and let's make
some delightful Christmas memories!

Minibooks from Word

Angels Billy Graham

The Applause of Heaven Max Lucado

The Be-Happy Attitudes Robert Schuller

He Still Moves Stones Max Lucado

In the Eye of the Storm Max Lucado

Laugh Again Charles Swindoll

Let's Make a Christmas Memory Gloria Gaither and
    Shirley Dobson

Motherhood Barbara Johnson

On Raising Children Mary Hollingsworth, compiler

Pack Up Your Gloomees Barbara Johnson

Parenting Isn't for Cowards James Dobson

Peace with God Billy Graham

Silver Boxes Florence Littauer

Splashes of Joy in the Cesspools of Life
    Barbara Johnson

Stick a Geranium in Your Hat and Be Happy Barbara
    Johnson

Together Forever Mary Hollingsworth, compiler

Unto the Hills Billy Graham